Croft & Dye Productions and Salt Lick Productions in association with
Neil McPherson for the Finborough Theatre presents

BY HARRY MCDONALD

Foam premiered at the Finborough Theatre, London,
on 19 March 2024.

f o a m

BY HARRY MCDONALD

Cast in order of speaking

Mosley	**Matthew Baldwin**
Nicky Crane	**Jake Richards**
Gabriel	**Kishore Walker**
Bird	**Keanu Adolphus Johnson**
Christopher	**Kishore Walker**
Craig	**Matthew Baldwin**
Nurse	**Keanu Adolphus Johnson**

Kent and London, 1974 to 1993.

The approximate running time is 85 minutes.
Please see front of house notices or ask an usher for an exact running time.
There will be no interval.

Director	**Matthew Iliffe**
Set Designer	**Nitin Parmar**
Costume Designer	**Pam Tait**
Lighting Designer	**Jonathan Chan**
Sound Designer	**David Segun Olowu**
Fight & Intimacy Director	**Jess Tucker Boyd**
Assistant Director	**Tania Khan**
Stage Manager	**Thomas Fielding**
Production Manager	**Carrie Croft**
Co-Producers	**Croft & Dye Productions**
	Salt Lick Productions

Face masks are optional, except on Covid Safe Sunday matinees when they are mandatory.

Please turn your mobile phones off – the light they emit can also be distracting.

Our patrons are respectfully reminded that, in this intimate theatre, any noise such as the rustling of programmes, food packaging or talking may distract the actors and your fellow audience members.

We regret that there is no admittance or readmittance to the auditorium whilst the performance is in progress.

Matthew Baldwin | Mosley / Craig

Theatre includes *The Act* (Trafalgar Studios), *46 Beacon* (Hope Theatre), *Outings* (Edinburgh Festival), *The Clouds* (ADC Cambridge), and many pantomimes including *Sleeping Beauty Takes A Prick* and eight other adult pantomimes (Above The Stag Theatre) and two seasons of family pantomimes (Queen's Theatre, Barnstaple).
Film includes *Greed*.
Television includes *Riviera, The Crown, EastEnders, The Act, Greed* and *The Dark Room*.
Writing includes *I Miss the War*, a monologue for Mark Gatiss' *Queers* series (BBC) and two plays co-written with Thomas Hescott – *The Act* (Trafalgar Studios, and filmed with Cyril Nri and Samuel Barnett), and *Outings* (co-written with Thomas Hescott) (Edinburgh Festival featuring Simon Callow, Mark Thomas, Jim Davidson and many others, National Tour and Lyric Theatre, West End).

Keanu Adolphus Johnson | Bird / Nurse

Trained at Italia Conti.
Theatre includes *Backstairs Billy* (Duke of York's Theatre), *Kinky Boots* (Queens Theatre, Hornchurch and New Wolsey Theatre, Ipswich), *Aladdin* (Kenneth More Theatre, Ilford), *Dick Whittington – A New Dick In Town* (Above The Stag Theatre), *Never Lost At Home* (New Wolsey Theatre, Ispwich), *Herons, Red Velvet* and *The Laramie Project* (Italia Conti) and *A Place For Me* (Lighthouse Theatre)

Jake Richards | Nicky Crane

Trained at Arts Ed where he was nominated for a Laurence Olivier Bursary Award and awarded the Leverhulme Arts Scholarship. Theatre includes *A Midsummer Night's Dream* (Changeling Theatre), *Germ Free Adolescent* (Bunker Theatre) and *This Wounded Island* (Theatre503). Television includes *The Larkins II*.

Kishore Walker | Gabriel / Christopher

Trained at Guildhall School of Music and Drama.
Theatre includes *Passing* (Park Theatre) and *The Boys Are Kissing* (Theatre503).
Television includes *Queenie* and *Doctors*.

Harry McDonald | Playwright
Harry McDonald's debut play, *Don't Smoke in Bed*, premiered at the 2023 VAULT Festival. His short fiction has been published by *Another North*, and he has also created work for the *Liverpool Everyman's Love Liverpool project*. Between 2016-2019, he published a blog of theatre criticism.

Matthew Iliffe | Director
Productions at the Finborough Theatre include *Bacon* for which he won an OffWestEnd Award for Best Director (Finborough Theatre, Riverside Studios, Summerhall Edinburgh, Bristol Old Vic and SoHo Playhouse, New York City), Eleanor Burgess' *The Niceties*, and Lionel Bart and Alun Owen's musical *Maggie May*. Direction includes *Breeding* (King's Head Theatre), *Four Play* (Above The Stag Theatre) and *The Burnt Part Boys* which was nominated for the OffWestEnd Award for Best Director and Best Musical Production (Park Theatre).
Assistant Direction includes assisting Polly Findlay on *Assassins* (Chichester Festival Theatre), Daniel Evans on *Black Superhero* (Royal Court Theatre), Hannah Chissick on *Brass* (National Youth Music Theatre at Hackney Empire) and as Associate Director on *Musik* (Leicester Square Theatre).
Matthew graduated from the University of Bristol with a first class honours degree in Theatre and Performance Studies, and trained on the National Theatre Directors Course 2023, and the StoneCrabs Young Directors Programme 2015.

Nitin Parmar | Set Design
Nitin is a Linbury Prize winner for Costume and Stage design 2023 and a 2022 MA graduate of Costume for Performance.
He is a multi disciplinary artist and designer and his work spans installations, stage and film.
His digital short films have been selected to be shown at Aesthetica Film Festival 2022 and for the launch of The Outernet London 2022
Film includes the upcoming Bong Joon-Ho film.

Pam Tait | Costume Design
Theatre include *Top Girls* (Royal Court Theatre) as well as touring work with Hull Truck, Monstrous Regiment, English Stage Company and Great Easter Stage.
Television include *Queer As Folk*, *In a Land of Plenty*, *Sid and Nancy*, *Pascali's Island*, *Beautiful Thing*.
Dance and cabaret include *Ballet of Nations* (Impermanence Dance Theatre) and work for Thick and Tight Dance, Screaming Alley Cabaret, and English National Ballet.

Jonathan Chan | Lighting Design
Productions at the Finborough Theatre include *The Straw Chair* and *Pussycat in Memory of Darkness*. Trained at the Guildhall School of Music and Drama.
Theatre includes *Ignition* (Frantic Assembly), *The Flea* (Yard Theatre), *Kim's Convenience*, *Candy* (Park Theatre), *Love Bomb* (National Youth Theatre), *Duck* (Arcola Theatre), *Grindr:The Opera* (Union Theatre), *All Roads* (London Tour), *In the Net* (Jermyn Street Theatre), *Grandad, Me and Teddy Too* (Polka Theatre), *Tiny Tim's Christmas Carol*, *She Stoops to Conquer, The Solid Life of Sugar Water* (Orange Tree Theatre), *Lady Dealer* (Paines Plough Roundabout), *An Interrogation* (Summerhall), *Emmeline* (national tour), *Heroin to Hero* (Edinburgh Fringe), *Move Fast and Break Things* (Camden People's Theatre and Edinburgh Fringe), *Get Happy* (Pleasance London), *Maybe Probably*, *Belvedere* and *Snowflakes* (Old Red Lion Theatre), *Different Owners at Sunrise* (Roundhouse), *Barstools to Broadway*

and *Amphibian* (King's Head Theatre), *Sticks and Stones*, *Time* and *Random* (Tristan Bates Theatre), *Siapa Yang Bawa Melayu Aku Pergi?* (*Who Took My Malay Away?*) (Network Theatre), *Don't Send Flowers* (White Bear Theatre), *Life of Olu* (Theatre Peckham and Golden Goose Theatre) and *Fester* (Cockpit Theatre and Bridge House Theatre). Associate and Assistant Lighting Design includes *The Passenger* (Guildhall School of Music and Drama) and *Fidelio* (Glyndebourne).

David Segun Olowu | Sound Design
David uses his background in music production to tell stories and craft intricate, immersive soundscapes using sound and music.
Theatre includes *What I Hear I Keep* (Talawa TYPT23).

Jess Tucker Boyd | Fight and Intimacy Director
Productions at the Finborough Theatre includes *Bacon* (Finborough Theatre, Riverside Studios, Bristol Old Vic and SoHo Playhouse, New York City).
Trained as an actor and theatre maker at East 15 Acting School, and in Movement Direction at the Royal Central School of Speech and Drama. Movement Direction includes *Hakawatis* (Shakespeare's Globe), *Katzenmusik* (Royal Court Theatre), *Come Inside* (Bush Theatre), *BU21* (Theatre503), *Moormaid* (Arcola Theatre), *Honeybee* (Pleasance Theatre) and *Gutted* (Marlowe Theatre, Canterbury).
Intimacy Coordination includes *One Day* (Drama Republic), *The Winter King* (Bad Wolf), *Dangerous Liaisons* (Playground Productions), *I Hate Suzy* (Bad Wolf and Sky Vision), *Missing Julie* (Theatr Clwyd) and *Faustus: That Damned Woman* (Lyric Theatre, Hammersmith).

Carrie Croft | Production Manager
Productions at the Finborough Theatre include *Birthright*.
Trained at Guildhall School of Music and Drama.
She is Resident Production Manager at Rose Bruford College.
Productions as Producer and Production Manager include *Priscilla the Party* (Here at Outernet), *The Realness* (Big House Theatre), *Othello* (Riverside Studios), *Disruption* and *The Shape of Things* (Park Theatre), *Apocalypse Bear Trilogy* (Jack Studio Theatre), *Love and Information* (Omnibus Theatre), *Fucking Men* (Waterloo East Theatre), *Breeding* (King's Head Theatre), *Earthquakes in London* and *Ring Ring* (Omnibus Theatre), *Under the Black Rock* (Arcola Theatre) and *Sus* (Park Theatre).

Thomas Fielding | Stage Manager
Trained at the Royal Academy of Dramatic Art.
Theatre includes *Picasso*, *Crime and Punishment*, *Snow White* (Theatre Royal, Bury St Edmunds) and *Cash Money Now!* (Big House Theatre).

Croft & Dye Productions | Producers
Productions at the Finborough Theatre include *Birthright*.
Theatre include *JULIE:The Musical* (national tour), *Tit Swingers* (The Other Palace), *The Shape of Things* (Park Theatre) and *Operation Epsilon* (Southwark Playhouse).

Production Acknowledgements
PR | **Kate Morley PR**
Promotional photography | **Ali Wright**
Lighting supplied by | **White Light**
Thanks to | **Caroline Molloy** at St Martin-in-the-Fields

FINBOROUGH THEATRE

'Probably the most influential fringe theatre in the world.'
Time Out

'Not just a theatre, but a miracle.' *Metro*

'The mighty little Finborough which, under Neil McPherson, continues to offer a mixture of neglected classics and new writing in a cannily curated mix.' Lyn Gardner, *The Stage*

'The tiny but mighty Finborough' Ben Brantley, *The New York Times*

Founded in 1980, the multi-award-winning Finborough Theatre presents plays and music theatre, concentrated exclusively on vibrant new writing and unique rediscoveries – both in our 1868 Victorian home and online with our digital initiative – #FinboroughFrontier

Our programme is unique – we never present work that has been seen anywhere in London during the last 25 years. Behind the scenes, we continue to discover and develop a new generation of theatre makers. Despite remaining completely unsubsidised, the Finborough Theatre has an unparalleled track record for attracting the finest talent who go on to become leading voices in British theatre. Under Artistic Director Neil McPherson, it has discovered some of the UK's most exciting new playwrights including Laura Wade, James Graham, Mike Bartlett, Jack Thorne, Carmen Nasr, Athena Stevens and Anders Lustgarten, and directors including Tamara Harvey, Robert Hastie, Tom Littler, Blanche McIntyre, Kate Wasserberg and Sam Yates.

Artists working at the theatre in the 1980s included Clive Barker, Rory Bremner, Nica Burns, Kathy Burke, Ken Campbell, Jane Horrocks, Nicola Walker and Claire Dowie. In the 1990s, the Finborough Theatre first became known for new writing including Naomi Wallace's first play *The War Boys*, Rachel Weisz in David Farr's *Neville Southall's Washbag*, four plays by Anthony Neilson including *Penetrator* and *The Censor*, both of which transferred to the Royal Court Theatre, and new plays by Richard Bean, Lucinda Coxon, David Eldridge and Tony Marchant. New writing development included the premieres of modern classics such as Mark Ravenhill's *Shopping and F***king*, Conor McPherson's *This Lime Tree Bower*, Naomi Wallace's *Slaughter City* and Martin McDonagh's *The Pillowman*.

Since 2000, new British plays have included Laura Wade's London debut *Young Emma* (commissioned by the Finborough Theatre), James Graham's London debut *Albert's Boy* with Victor Spinetti and four other of his first plays, Sarah Grochala's *S27*, Athena Stevens' *Schism* which was nominated for an Olivier Award, West End transfers for Joy Wilkinson's *Fair*, Nicholas de Jongh's *Plague*

Over England, Jack Thorne's *Fanny and Faggot*, Neil McPherson's Olivier Award nominated *It Is Easy To Be Dead*, and Dawn King's *Foxfinder*, and a New York transfer for Sophie Swithinbank's *Bacon*.

UK premieres of foreign plays have included plays by Lanford Wilson, Larry Kramer, Tennessee Williams, Suzan-Lori Parks, the English premieres of two Scots language classics by Robert McLellan, and more Canadian plays than any other theatre in Europe, with West End transfers for Frank McGuinness' *Gates of Gold* with William Gaunt, Craig Higginson's *Dream of the Dog* with Dame Janet Suzman and Jordan Tannahill's *Late Company*. In December 2022, the Finborough Theatre became the first foreign theatre to perform in Ukraine since the Russian invasion with *Pussycat in Memory of Darkness* which has subsequently revisited Kyiv, and played in Germany and the USA.

Rediscoveries of neglected work – most commissioned by the Finborough Theatre – have included the first London revivals of Rolf Hochhuth's *Soldiers* and *The Representative*, both parts of Keith Dewhurst's *Lark Rise to Candleford*, *Etta Jenks* with Clarke Peters and Daniela Nardini, three rediscoveries from Noël Coward, Terence Rattigan's *Variation On A Theme* with Rachael Stirling, and Lennox Robinson's *Drama at Inish* with Celia Imrie and Paul O'Grady. Transfers have included Emlyn Williams' *Accolade*, John Van Druten's *London Wall*, and J. B. Priestley's *Cornelius* which had a sell-out Off-Broadway run in New York City.

Music Theatre has included the new and the old, including the acclaimed 'Celebrating British Music Theatre' series, with West End transfers for Adam Gwon's *Ordinary Days* and the UK premiere of Rodgers and Hammerstein's *State Fair*. Specially curated playlists of Finborough Theatre music theatre are available to listen to for free on Spotify.

The Finborough Theatre won the 2020 and 2022 London Pub Theatres Pub Theatre of the Year Award, *The Stage* Fringe Theatre of the Year Award in 2011, the Empty Space Peter Brook Award in 2010 and 2012 and nominated in 2023, and was nominated for an Olivier Award in 2017 and 2019. Artistic Director Neil McPherson was awarded the Critics' Circle Special Award for Services to Theatre in 2019. It is the only unsubsidised theatre ever to be awarded the Channel 4 Playwrights Scheme bursary twelve times.

www.finboroughtheatre.co.uk

FINBOROUGH THEATRE

118 Finborough Road, London SW10 9ED
admin@finboroughtheatre.co.uk
www.finboroughtheatre.co.uk

The Finborough Theatre is a member of the Independent Theatre Council, the Society of Independent Theatres, Musical Theatre Network, The Friends of Brompton Cemetery, The Earl's Court Society, The Kensington Society, and the WEST Theatre Association, Kyiv, Ukraine.

Supported by

The Finborough Theatre has the support of the Peggy Ramsay Foundation / Film 4 Playwrights Awards Scheme.

Mailing
Email admin@finboroughtheatre.co.uk or give your details to our Box Office staff to join our free email list.

Playscripts
Many of the Finborough Theatre's plays have been published and are on sale from our website.

Environment
The Finborough Theatre has a 100% sustainable electricity supply.

Local History
The Finborough Theatre's local history website is online at
www.earlscourtlocalhistory.co.uk

The Finborough Theatre on social media
www.facebook.com/FinboroughTheatre
www.twitter.com/finborough
www.instagram.com/finboroughtheatre
www.youtube.com/@finboroughtheatre
www.tiktok.com/@finboroughtheatre
www.threads.net/@finboroughtheatre
Search 'Finborough Theatre' on Spotify for specially curated playlists

Friends of the Finborough Theatre
The Finborough Theatre is a registered charity. We receive no public funding, and rely solely on the support of our audiences.
Please do consider supporting us by joining our Friends of the Finborough Theatre scheme.
There are five categories of Friends, each offering a wide range of benefits. Please ask any member of our staff for a leaflet.
William Terriss Friends – Anonymous. Catrin Evans. Anne and Patrick Foster. Janet and Leo Liebster. Ros and Alan Haigh.
Adelaide Neilson Friends – Charles Glanville. Philip G Hooker.
Legacy Gifts – Tom Erhardt.

Smoking is not permitted in the auditorium.
The videotaping or making of electronic or other audio and/or visual recordings or streams of this production is strictly prohibited.
There is no admittance or readmittance into the auditorium whilst the performance is in progress.

In accordance with the requirements of the Royal Borough of Kensington and Chelsea:
1. The public may leave at the end of the performance by all doors and such doors must at that time be kept open.
2. All gangways, corridors, staircases and external passageways intended for exit shall be left entirely free from obstruction whether permanent or temporary.
3. Persons shall not be permitted to stand or sit in any of the gangways intercepting the seating or to sit in any of the other gangways.

The Finborough Theatre is a registered charity and a company limited by guarantee. Registered in England and Wales no. 03448268. Registered Charity no. 1071304. Registered Office: 118 Finborough Road, London SW10 9ED.

FOAM

Harry McDonald

Yes, all men are homosexual, some turn straight. It must be very odd to be a straight man because your sexuality is hopelessly defensive. It's like an ideal of racial purity.

Derek Jarman, At Your Own Risk

As I look ahead, I am filled with foreboding. Like the Roman, I seem to see 'the River Tiber foaming with much blood'.

Enoch Powell, Birmingham, 20th April 1968

Characters

NICKY
MOSLEY
GABRIEL
BIRD
CHRISTOPHER
CRAIG
A NURSE

Notes

The play takes place in a series of public bathrooms.

BIRD and the NURSE are characters with Black African or
Caribbean heritage.

A slash (/) indicates where the next line interrupts.

A comma (,) on its own line indicates a beat or a pause,
dependent on context.

*This text went to press before the end of rehearsals and so may
differ slightly from the play as performed.*

ONE

April 1974.

NICKY, *a boy of fifteen, is shaving his head with a razor over the sink.*

MOSLEY, *an elegantly dressed aristocrat in his late thirties, has just walked into the bathroom carrying a cherry-red gift bag. He sets it down on the floor. He takes off his gloves.*

,

MOSLEY. Yes. They said that you had shaved your head. I did not realise they meant right this very second. Over the sink.

,

Excuse me a moment.

MOSLEY *crosses to a urinal. Unzips.*

,

Finishes, shakes, zips up again. Turns back to NICKY.

May I borrow the sink for a moment?

,

I need to wash my hands.

NICKY *steps away. Shaving foam drips down his face.*

Thank you.

MOSLEY *washes his hands. Carefully dries them.*

And your name is…?

NICKY. why are you talking

,

MOSLEY. I was asking you a question

NICKY. people don't talk in here

MOSLEY. of course

NICKY. they don't

MOSLEY. And yet I am.

NICKY. do you not know the rules or something

MOSLEY. of course I know the rules. I know the idiosyncrasies of a place like this.

NICKY. the what

MOSLEY. Idiosyncrasies. That which renders something abnormal. Like your new hair, or lack thereof.

NICKY. I'm not fucking strange

MOSLEY. You appear to have set about shaving your head over the sink in a public lavatory. If you are not strange then what, exactly, are you?

,

NICKY. what do you want

MOSLEY. answer my question and I shall see how I feel about answering yours.

NICKY. I don't do names

MOSLEY. Perhaps you could learn to.

,

NICKY. My name's Nicky. What do you want?

MOSLEY. My name is Mosley. Nice to meet you.

He holds out his hand.

You can shake it.

,

Shake my hand.

,

NICKY *does*.

Good. Not a terrible handshake either. Young men like you often have a limp handshake.

,

NICKY. who said I'd shaved my head

MOSLEY. I presumed they were your friends. That particular gaggle of boys.

NICKY. what boys

MOSLEY. I overhead them / talking

NICKY. you a perv?

,

MOSLEY. Excuse me? No I am not / a

NICKY. you look like a perv

MOSLEY. I am not a perv.

NICKY. if you're not a perv then what do you want

MOSLEY. I thought it was quite evident I am here to use the facilities. As are you. Though I suspect there is something else.

NICKY. It's quiet

MOSLEY. right.

NICKY. it *was* quiet

MOSLEY. and you do like the quiet.

NICKY. why are you still talking

MOSLEY. Because you seem like a nice boy and I would like to talk to you, and I think perhaps we should be sweeping aside conventions if they stand in the way of my doing so.

,

And you do like the quiet?

,

You can trust me.

NICKY *scoffs*.

You can. And you hardly seem in a hurry to leave so we might as well have a conversation. Or failing a conversation, perhaps you can listen to me. Here –

MOSLEY *offers* NICKY *a cigarette*.

I am sure you would like one of these.

,

NICKY *takes it.* MOSLEY *offers him a lighter, a fancy, heavy silver one.*

NICKY *doesn't know how to use it.*

MOSLEY *lights* NICKY's *cigarette, and then one for himself.* NICKY *tries to contain his cough.* MOSLEY *pretends not to notice.*

,

Yes. You are right. It is quiet. Quiet but not… Quiet as if something might happen.

NICKY. I like the quiet.

MOSLEY. *Why* do you like the quiet, Nicky.

,

NICKY. don't get much of it

MOSLEY. and why is that

NICKY. so many questions

MOSLEY. We can blame my insatiably curious mind.

NICKY *stares at his cigarette.*

NICKY. there's lots of noise at home.

MOSLEY. I see. Are there rather a lot of you?

,

NICKY. Ten of us. Including me.

MOSLEY. Yes. That must be difficult. Rather a lot of noise.

NICKY. yeah

MOSLEY. Not the right conditions for a young man. Trying to make sense of this bright shiny new world. And his place in it.

,

I have not been to this particular establishment before but I am familiar with the kind. And you are right of course. People keep their mouths wired shut. Until, of course, someone wants it open.

NICKY. it's a toilet

MOSLEY. yes.

,

NICKY. it's a toilet

MOSLEY. yes, but, I wonder –

MOSLEY disappears inside a cubicle. Closes the door over.

Yes!

A finger appears through a hole in the door. MOSLEY *re-emerges, proud of his discovery.*

Slightly more discreet than some. Not large enough for the obvious but perfectly effective.

NICKY. what

MOSLEY. A perfectly effective peephole.

,

Fewer and fewer of this kind around. They are good for the quiet. And other things – patience, for one. That necessary agony. The act of learning to wait for something to happen and then not being too disappointed when nothing happens at all. You do know what I mean. The kind of man that comes into a public lavatory for the quiet. And then its release.

,

NICKY. what do you want

MOSLEY. How old are you?

,

NICKY. Nineteen.

MOSLEY. yes I imagine that works with most people.

,

NICKY. Sixteen.

,

Fifteen.

MOSLEY. Yes that sounds about right. Looks older but still silly enough to, well… shave his head in a public lavatory.

NICKY. sixteen next month

MOSLEY. How very vibrant.

NICKY. vibrant

MOSLEY. Yes. Vital. Crucial. Shiny.

NICKY. how old are you?

MOSLEY. well. What year is this?

NICKY. seventy-four.

MOSLEY. Nineteen seventy-four? I suppose that puts me at seventy-seven years old.

,

What made you want to shave your head?

NICKY. I like how it looks

MOSLEY. *I* like how it looks too but that is not necessarily enough to make me go and shave my hair off, is it.

NICKY. I like how it looks on other people

MOSLEY. and you want to be like them?

NICKY. they look good. They look. Like they know what they're doing and they look good together. And I want to be like them.

,

MOSLEY. It is not just as simple as shaving your head though. If it were that simple everyone would do it.

NICKY. not everyone wants to do it

MOSLEY. No. Do you wonder why that is?

NICKY. they're not like me

MOSLEY. Precisely. It is because they are not like you. They are not like me either. Those boys, the ones you want to look like. Well, I happen to know them and their ilk quite well.

NICKY. really

MOSLEY. Men of rigour and action. Once I am finished with them, at least.

   MOSLEY *stubs out whatever's left of his cigarette.* NICKY *copies him.*

NICKY. how do you know them

MOSLEY. I run a club. I suppose it is a… social gathering for young men like you to get to know each other. To learn new skills. To have fun.

NICKY. what sort of fun

   ,

MOSLEY. There are sports teams, for instance. Does that sort of thing interest you?

   ,

NICKY. what sports

MOSLEY. There are football teams, cricket teams. The boxing club is very popular too.

NICKY. I like boxing.

MOSLEY. Ah, do you really?

NICKY. yeah

MOSLEY. Do you just spectate or do you like to get stuck in

NICKY. I get

   NICKY *smirks into his shoulder.*

MOSLEY. What is it?

NICKY. I get proper stuck in

MOSLEY. Quite right too.

NICKY. yeah I like it when they watch

   ,

MOSLEY. Really.

NICKY. yeah. Is that weird?

MOSLEY. No, not at all. You like it when they watch?

   ,

   You can tell me what you like, Nicky.

NICKY. yeah

MOSLEY. You like it when they watch you, when they admire you

NICKY. yeah

MOSLEY. when they are worshipping you

   ,

NICKY. no one ha, no one worships me

MOSLEY. But they could do. Who knows.

NICKY. do you?

MOSLEY. Do I what.

   ,

   Like to be watched?

   ,

NICKY. do you box

   ,

MOSLEY. Yes. Yes, as a matter of fact I do box.

NICKY. you don't look the type.

MOSLEY. True. But types can be deceiving. It can be good to compartmentalise, to carve yourself into discrete pieces. They can be quite separate. But all very much real.

,

I think you should come along some time.

NICKY. I don't really do clubs.

,

MOSLEY. I think you would like this one.

,

You can trust me you know.

NICKY. right

MOSLEY. You are uptight. Unnecessarily so. You just need to relax. Take a deep breath.

MOSLEY *reaches into his pocket and retrieves a bottle of poppers. He tosses them to* NICKY *who makes no attempt to catch them.*

You were supposed to catch them

NICKY *picks them up.*

NICKY. what

MOSLEY. They will help you relax.

NICKY. I don't know what they are.

MOSLEY. Here –

MOSLEY *takes them, unscrews the lid and raises the bottle to his own nostril, closing the other with a finger. Then he puts the bottle under* NICKY*'s nostril, closing the other with a finger.*

You just breathe in, and it does the rest, hardly complicated.

NICKY *takes a deep breath.*

And how is that?

NICKY. yeah

MOSLEY *screws the lid back on.*

MOSLEY. See? You can trust me.

,

NICKY *kisses* MOSLEY *impulsively.*

,

NICKY. sorry

MOSLEY. No. Not that. Never apologise. Not ever. If that is what you want, you cannot ever apologise for it.

,

Is that what you want, Nicky?

,

NICKY. yeah.

,

MOSLEY. what on earth are you scared of?

,

NICKY. I'm not a queer.

MOSLEY. a what

NICKY. not a queer.

,

MOSLEY. ah. I see. And yet.

MOSLEY *tosses him the poppers again.* NICKY *catches them.*

Good boy.

NICKY *unscrews the lid, takes another hit of poppers.*

Oh. A quick learner.

NICKY *pockets the poppers.*

NICKY. Mine now.

,

MOSLEY. Oh I like you very much.

,

There is a world that belongs to you. Men of intellect,
energy, craftsmanship and skill. And yet you are expected to
sit around idle, waiting, instead of setting about taking it by
yourself. And you have no idea, because you are still pink in
the cheeks and undercooked.

NICKY. what do you mean pink

MOSLEY *is close enough for* NICKY *to touch him.*

MOSLEY. You must march in. You must say whatever it is
that you want to say. You must laugh in the face of any
opposition. You must scream that the opposition is denying
you what you are in fact perfectly entitled to and you must
do that for what will feel like a very long time and then once
you have run out of that kind of patience, you must beat
whatever resistance you meet into the gutter. I have given my
life to it. It has a name. It is called Fascism. It is a creed of
love and of self-sacrifice. And it needs you.

,

NICKY. I can do that

MOSLEY. can you?

NICKY. yes.

MOSLEY. Prove it.

NICKY *takes his vest off. Tries to look threatening.*

,

Yes. Pink.

NICKY. you are a perv

MOSLEY. Hm. Maybe. I have something else for you.

NICKY's eyeing the bag.

NICKY. how many presents you got?

MOSLEY. I had almost forgotten about this one –

He holds out the bag.

This is for you.

NICKY takes the bag. Inside the bag is a shoebox, and inside the shoebox, resting on red tissue paper, is a pair of cherry-red boots. NICKY holds them up to the light.

NICKY. these are for me?

MOSLEY. I think they'll suit you.

NICKY kicks his shoes off. Pulls the boots on. MOSLEY watches.

MOSLEY kneels down and ties NICKY's laces.

,

NICKY. happy now?

MOSLEY. Yes. As a matter of fact I am.

MOSLEY reaches out to touch NICKY's head.

May I?

NICKY nods. MOSLEY takes NICKY's chin in his hand, manoeuvres his head around. He's inspecting him.

NICKY. do you ever worry people might walk in

MOSLEY. No.

NICKY. not ever

MOSLEY. No.

,

Show me your teeth.

NICKY *bares his teeth.* MOSLEY *runs a finger across them.*

Good boy.

He removes his finger. Wipes it on a paper towel.

Turn around. Give me a twirl.

,

NICKY *rotates, slowly.*

Are you a Nicholas?

NICKY. Nicola.

MOSLEY. Ah. Hardly an Anglo-Saxon name.

NICKY. what

MOSLEY. Not an English name.

NICKY. My mum's Italian.

MOSLEY. ah, I enjoy Italy. I spent a lot of time there with some friends of mine. I enjoy young men like you. But you do understand that there is a difference between us?

NICKY. I'm not / stupid

MOSLEY. unlike you, Nicky, they will never call *me* a *queer.*

MOSLEY *slips his hand down the front of* NICKY*'s trousers.*

,

What? That was the word you used.

NICKY. I –

MOSLEY. What?

NICKY. I'm not a queer.

MOSLEY *withdraws his hand, shoves* NICKY *away lightly.*

I'm not.

MOSLEY. of course not. Then what are you?

,

NICKY *swings for* MOSLEY. MOSLEY *catches his hand, puts his other round* NICKY*'s neck.*

Now then. Playing silly little games is for silly little boys.

NICKY. not playing games

MOSLEY *slides* NICKY*'s reluctant hand down the front of his trousers.*

MOSLEY. There. That is more like it.

MOSLEY *laughs.* NICKY *grabs and twists –*

MOSLEY *howls –*

NICKY *is free, throws a punch – they scrap –*

little shit

NICKY. let me go

MOSLEY. oh come on then, what exactly are you?

NICKY *breaks* MOSLEY*'s nose –*

FUCK. FUCKING FUCK.

,

Ow.

NICKY *catches his breath.* MOSLEY *stems the bleeding.*

NICKY. You've got blood on my boots.

MOSLEY. Oh I do apologise.

NICKY. Get it off.

,

MOSLEY. What?

NICKY. I said get it off

,

MOSLEY. No.

NICKY. Yes.

MOSLEY. queer

NICKY. perv

MOSLEY. scum

NICKY. posh cunt

   MOSLEY *laughs*.

MOSLEY. yes I do like you very much indeed.

   ,

NICKY. You deaf or something? You got blood on my boots.

MOSLEY. I do apologise.

NICKY. Get the blood. Off my boots.

   ,

MOSLEY. What on earth do you think I am?

NICKY. Don't care about that. It's what I want.

   NICKY *throws some toilet paper at him*.

   ,

   MOSLEY *starts to wipe at the boots with the toilet paper.
   The blood doesn't shift*.

   He spits on the shoes, rubs again.

   MOSLEY *licks the boots*.

   Good boy.

   ,

   MOSLEY *stands up. He laughs. He wipes his nose in the
   mirror*.

MOSLEY. Yes. You are going to do very well indeed. You
   should come to the club. Make some friends.

   *He strides out of the bathroom with as much dignity as he
   can muster*.

TWO

June 1978.

The bathroom door swings shut behind GABRIEL.

He is sober, NICKY *is not.*

NICKY. That was good! That was really fucking good

GABRIEL. yeah it was

NICKY. that was so good

GABRIEL. it was great

NICKY. it was fucking brilliant – that crowd – fuck me

GABRIEL. they were into it

NICKY. I would quite happily get off with every single one of those beautiful bastards out there and I don't care how long it would take. You could blink and every time you opened your eyes I'd have my tongue in someone else's mouth

GABRIEL. okay

NICKY. I could have crowd surfed I should have crowd surfed there's no way they would have dropped me they were so into it

GABRIEL. yeah no they wouldn't have dropped you

NICKY. second half of the set I am going to crowd surf and they are not going to drop me

GABRIEL. no

NICKY. and I am going to get off with every single one of them

GABRIEL. right

NICKY. I am a GOD tonight

GABRIEL *laughs*.

what are you laughing at

GABRIEL. I'm not laughing

NICKY. You were laughing

GABRIEL. no no not laughing

,

NICKY. You were. I saw you.

,

Kidding. Don't look so worried. Just fun innit. But I am so crowd surfing later. And I do intend on snogging quite a lot of fucking people.

GABRIEL. That seems more achievable.

NICKY. fuck me I want another drink.

NICKY *unzips his jeans, reaches into the crotch –*

GABRIEL. oh –

Pulls out two miniatures of vodka and throws one at GABRIEL.

I can't, I really can't

NICKY *cracks open the lid.*

NICKY. *Cheers.*

NICKY *downs the vodka.* GABRIEL *manages about half of his before coughing.*

I don't have any mixers on me, ran out of room.

GABRIEL. That's, that's fine. I'm fine. I'm fine.

,

NICKY. think I'm still high

GABRIEL. probably that's likely yes

NICKY. I'm so fucking, like, up there

GABRIEL. You look it. In a good way

NICKY. I think if you're the frontman in a band you should always look like you're on the verge of passing out in your own vomit

GABRIEL. oh okay

NICKY. it's punk

GABRIEL. sure

NICKY. well I say punk, punk's dead isn't it

GABRIEL. yeah maybe

NICKY. they're all fucking commies, haven't got a clue

,

who are you?

GABRIEL. oh I'm no one I'm just here

NICKY. I can see that

GABRIEL. it doesn't matter

NICKY. what's your name?

GABRIEL. Gabriel.

NICKY. what like the

GABRIEL. yes like the and yes I've heard / all the

NICKY. no no wasn't gonna make jokes. Promise. It's a nice name.

GABRIEL. thanks

NICKY. and, like, what are you doing here. In here

GABRIEL. what do you mean

NICKY. you followed me

GABRIEL. you asked me to follow you

NICKY. when

GABRIEL. just now, when you finished

NICKY. oh

GABRIEL. you called me camera-boy

NICKY. OH

GABRIEL *waves his camera.*

GABRIEL. which is among the nicer things I get called on the job

NICKY. the camera-boy, yeah, yeah I remember, you look different in bathroom light

GABRIEL. everyone looks different in bathroom light

NICKY. I mean you look great I'm just saying

GABRIEL. no no it's great for photos

NICKY. did you get many tonight?

GABRIEL. That's what I'm here for.

NICKY. oh so you are on the job? I thought you were just carrying it around. Like for fun or something

GABRIEL. No no. Working. Wave a camera about you'll get in anywhere. You should try it some time.

NICKY. nah I'd break it

GABRIEL. what, are you that clumsy

NICKY. nah it's my instinct to smash shit up

GABRIEL. sure.

,

you see all sorts of things doing this

NICKY. yeah I bet

GABRIEL. this is my fourth club tonight

NICKY. you *slag*

GABRIEL *laughs*.

GABRIEL. yeah

,

NICKY. So where have you been tonight?

GABRIEL. Paradise. Queens Court. Rockies. Now here. Then the day job tomorrow. Today. In a few hours.

NICKY. and you're sober

GABRIEL. yeah

NICKY. maybe you shouldn't be

GABRIEL. that wouldn't end well

NICKY. what, have you done it before, turned up pissed or
    something

GABRIEL. well yeah when I started there was a night / when I

NICKY. All gay places

GABRIEL. what

NICKY. Paradise, Queens Court, Rockies.

GABRIEL. Yeah

NICKY. they all play disco

GABRIEL. Yeah. I mean, it pays. I don't turn down a gig

NICKY. me neither

GABRIEL. but it's good fun

NICKY. Mr In-Demand, meant to be my job tonight

GABRIEL. no no I just mean

NICKY. I'm kidding. Stop worrying.

GABRIEL. it's just

NICKY. what

GABRIEL. nothing you're just

NICKY. just what

,

GABRIEL. you know there's so much going on at the moment.
    Like all these clubs, new nights, new bars and all the new
    people there and it's buzzing and they barely notice I'm
    there but I notice them and then the photos are great because
    they're not posing and the photo is actually of them

,

    sorry I'm rambling I'm boring / you

NICKY. no it's nice

GABRIEL. I like my job

NICKY. how many people'd fucking say that

GABRIEL. that's true

NICKY. yeah wouldn't bother feeling sorry for yourself

   GABRIEL *laughs*.

GABRIEL. ha no, no I don't. I'm good.

   ,

NICKY. Have you taken many photos tonight

GABRIEL. Yeah quite a few

   ,

NICKY. Have you taken many photos of me

GABRIEL. Yeah. A few.

   ,

NICKY. You haven't asked me my name?

GABRIEL. I know your name

   ,

   You're Nicky. You announced it onstage. Hundreds of people
   cheered when you introduced yourself

NICKY. Nice to meet you.

   He holds his hand out.

GABRIEL. We're shaking hands?

   ,

   GABRIEL *shakes his hand.*

NICKY. I'm a civilised gent. You say the lighting in bathrooms
   is good?

GABRIEL. yeah everyone looks good in bathroom light

NICKY. and that isn't just because everyone's high. Or like
   bleary eyed from the lights out there. I don't know that I
   believe you

GABRIEL. I'm not high

NICKY. maybe you should put that thing to some use then. Get to work, camera-boy

GABRIEL. you gonna give me something to work with?

,

Your fly's still undone, by the way

NICKY. oh you noticed

GABRIEL. got a good eye.

> NICKY *slowly zips up his jeans.* GABRIEL *raises the camera and takes a photograph.*

NICKY. You went for an action shot.

GABRIEL. is that your idea of action?

NICKY. a little bit

GABRIEL. try draping yourself over the sink. See if you look all tragic and vulnerable and everything that works for the punk zines

NICKY. tragic and vulnerable

GABRIEL. yes

NICKY. what the fuck is that

GABRIEL. I think that's what they go for

> NICKY *drapes himself over the sink. He doesn't look particularly tragic or vulnerable.* GABRIEL *takes a photograph.*

,

NICKY. That was shit wasn't it

GABRIEL. not my best work to be honest. It's, you're posing. Yeah no it's never good when people pose. Maybe you shouldn't pose for me.

NICKY. why not

GABRIEL. Just feels forced. Like you want me to know that you know I'm there. Like if you'd fallen on the sink it might look good but you didn't fall because I told you to drape

NICKY. right

GABRIEL. If that makes sense

NICKY. not really

GABRIEL. Oh

NICKY. do you ever take photos of yourself?

GABRIEL. fuck no

NICKY. just asking

GABRIEL. sorry I just no the thought would never

NICKY. why not?

GABRIEL. I'm just not a fan of me

NICKY. I would have thought you'd be a great model

GABRIEL. no

> ,

shut up

NICKY. But you must get looks in those places. In Paradise, Queens Court, Rockies. You must get some attention.

GABRIEL. I'm not like you

NICKY. you don't need to be. You're not looking at it when you get it, clearly. I bet there's people who'd want a photograph of you

GABRIEL. not on their bedroom wall

NICKY. maybe I would

> GABRIEL *laughs*.

I do I think you're very pretty.

> ,

GABRIEL. are you

> ,

NICKY. am I what

,

    Am I what?

GABRIEL. doesn't matter

NICKY. are you?

GABRIEL. yes

NICKY. like really

GABRIEL. yes

,

    you get to be so many things if your answer to every question is always yes.

NICKY. sounds fun

GABRIEL. why I love London.

NICKY. oh yeah?

GABRIEL. You can be as many different people as you want to be as long as you can still pay the rent.

    NICKY *rummages inside his jacket, finds a bag of coke.*

NICKY. Thank fuck.

    He tips out some coke onto the surface by the sink.

    Have you got a card or something?

GABRIEL. Like a business card

NICKY. I mean if that's all you've got then yeah it'll do

GABRIEL. Right. No, no I don't

,

NICKY. okay fine I'll suffer

    He snorts some coke.

    You want some?

GABRIEL. no, no thank you

NICKY. You still taking photos?

GABRIEL. Not of this

NICKY. Why not?

GABRIEL. It's not that you don't look good or anything it's more that I don't think the magazines I shoot for are going to publish a photo of you doing coke

NICKY. do they not

GABRIEL. no not really

NICKY. fucking boring

GABRIEL. You okay?

NICKY. I'm fine

GABRIEL. just you look a bit

NICKY. I get a bit nervous

GABRIEL. What like stage fright

NICKY. no it's not quite like that it's more like what if I'm shit

GABRIEL. you're not shit you just killed that first set, people loved it

NICKY. the next one though I could be shit the next one doesn't matter, doesn't matter, I'll be onstage with those songs I like singing those songs

GABRIEL. I like watching you when you're up there. You look like you're so in control. I mean you *are* in control. You've got all of us in the palm of your hand. You could tell us to do anything you wanted and there are hundreds of people out there right now who would do it.

,

Can I tell you something

NICKY. sure

GABRIEL. This place wasn't on my list of jobs tonight. This isn't a gay club, the photos I take here won't get printed, they're for me. The magazine's too interested in whether or not Barbara Windsor was at the last place. Which she was. But I'd heard about you. I wanted to meet you. I wanted you inside my camera. Just a piece of you.

NICKY. who told you about me

GABRIEL. mate of mine. Was a skinhead. Likes the look but changes it up when he gets bored. When I saw him last his hair had grown back, he said he'd just shaved it for a while. But he told me about some of the gigs he'd been to. And that you, that you were the real deal. That you keep it shaved. That your tattoos are real. And the lyrics aren't just to shock people. That you meant them.

NICKY. Yeah. Course I mean them.

,

GABRIEL. You know normally people deny that. Not a Nazi band! We're apolitical! We just like the look!

NICKY. everyone looks like a Nazi band it's part of the look

,

what

,

what are you looking at me like that for

GABRIEL. I'm just looking. Where I'm happiest.

,

NICKY. You can join in if you really want to.

GABRIEL. I'm fine where I am.

NICKY. Much more fun over here.

,

Come here.

,

GABRIEL *walks towards* NICKY. NICKY *kisses* GABRIEL *who almost drops the camera but catches it without breaking the kiss.*

How's that for an action shot

GABRIEL. Shut up

GABRIEL *kisses* NICKY – NICKY *picks up* GABRIEL *and sits him on the sink. He wraps his legs around* NICKY.

Do you want to fuck me?

NICKY. yeah

GABRIEL. you can fuck me if you want to

NICKY. yeah

GABRIEL. you can do anything you want to me

NICKY *pulls away.*

NICKY. Fuck's sake.

,

I can't. Not now. Got to go soon.

GABRIEL. yeah course.

He hops down from the sink, checks himself in the mirror.

I mean you could. You could totally fuck me right now.

NICKY. no.

GABRIEL. like anyone would care, like you care

NICKY. I haven't

GABRIEL. what. With anyone or just

,

NICKY. with someone like you

,

GABRIEL. Do I look like I just got necked by a Nazi?

NICKY. why, does that look different

GABRIEL. feels like it maybe should

NICKY. does it?

GABRIEL *looks in the mirror.*

GABRIEL. don't know

NICKY. I have to go. Second set.

GABRIEL. Of course. I'll be there. Camera-boy.

NICKY. I'll give you something to photograph

GABRIEL. You don't have to give me anything. I'll find it.

NICKY. There's some good ones in the / second set

GABRIEL. do you know what they are, the people that have paid to see you. Your fans.

,

NICKY. what are you trying to do

GABRIEL. I'm not trying to do anything

NICKY. you trying to shock me

GABRIEL. I think that would be pointless

NICKY. you trying to shame me?

GABRIEL. I think that would be impossible.

,

NICKY. what did you think?

GABRIEL. of what

NICKY. Of me. Of the set.

GABRIEL. I liked it

NICKY. you liked me?

GABRIEL. Yes

NICKY. Even with me being a Nazi?

,

GABRIEL. Well it's a look isn't it. It's not real it's just a look. It's a really fucking good way to shock people and I like that because once you've shocked someone you can do anything can't you

NICKY. suppose

GABRIEL. Like it doesn't have to mean anything does it

NICKY. did you think it was hot

GABRIEL. I don't know if. If I found it hot.

NICKY. You were wrapping your legs around me five minutes ago

GABRIEL. Not because of that

NICKY. Then why

GABRIEL. Because. I don't know it's none of my business now you're offstage. You know. Pay no attention to the man behind the curtain!

,

NICKY. What?

GABRIEL. Nothing just like. You're off duty.

NICKY. You just said it yourself. I'm the real deal

GABRIEL. But not like. Really.

,

NICKY. where do you think the ticket money goes

GABRIEL. your coke habit?

NICKY. from the club. Where do you think the money goes

GABRIEL. I wouldn't know

NICKY. you're part of it gorgeous.

,

GABRIEL. who are those people out there

NICKY. they're my fans

GABRIEL. are they all Nazis do you think or is it just some of them

NICKY. You don't / get it at all

GABRIEL. and if it is only some of them what does it say about the rest that they're happy to be going to a gig with Nazis and singing along to the same songs as them

NICKY. there's always people in the room you're not going to like

GABRIEL. if there are enough people in a room there's bound to be some Nazis, is that what you're saying

NICKY. well yeah

,

Do you like it?

GABRIEL. what do you mean do I like it

NICKY. Do you like it?

,

GABRIEL. do I like

NICKY. Yeah. Do you *like* it.

GABRIEL. a bit. I like how it looks. I like how it feels

NICKY. alright

NICKY *clicks his heels together and throws his right arm into a salute.*

Sieg Heil!

,

See. The sky didn't fall in. A fucking avalanche didn't crash through the window. Do you like it?

,

GABRIEL. Do it again.

> NICKY *clicks his heels together and throws his right arm into a salute.*

NICKY. Sieg Heil!

GABRIEL. again

NICKY. Sieg Heil

GABRIEL. again

NICKY. Sieg Heil

> GABRIEL *takes a photograph.*

,

GABRIEL. what

NICKY. do I look good?

GABRIEL. Yes.

NICKY. do you like it?

,

GABRIEL. Yes.

,

NICKY. I have to go. Second set.

GABRIEL. yeah. See you out there. I'll be watching.

> GABRIEL *goes.* NICKY *goes to follow him –*

THREE

September 1986.

The gents in a gay bar. The throb of disco in the walls.

NICKY *pushes* BIRD *– bleached jeans, Docs, white vest – inside.*

NICKY *props open a 'cleaning in progress' floor sign, places it outside the bathroom, then shuts the door and locks it behind him.*

They stare at each other.

BIRD. I am missing Diana Ross.

NICKY. yeah

BIRD. I can hear it.

NICKY. Yeah. Nice place this

BIRD. it's quite literally a shithole

NICKY. the grouting looks good.

BIRD. I can't say I'm a connoisseur.

NICKY. What do you want?

BIRD. here on a night out aren't I

NICKY. why

BIRD. because that's what gay men do on a Tuesday.

NICKY. who are you with

BIRD. my friends

NICKY. how many of them

BIRD. there's, what, five of us

NICKY. you planning on causing trouble

BIRD. my GOD I will scream this place down I will I will scream this place down if I don't get to go home with someone tonight because you have kept me in the fucking bog.

,

NICKY. how long were you in for?

BIRD. long enough to miss the dulcet tones of Miss Diana Ross

NICKY. how long

BIRD. you remember me then

NICKY. yeah I do

BIRD. need to have a word with management don't I. Fascists on the door. Not a good look.

NICKY. how long

,

BIRD. four years

,

NICKY. doesn't seem so bad

BIRD. not to you, you've not been out long yourself right

NICKY. what do you mean

BIRD. Residing at Her Majesty's pleasure. Not been out long, surely?

NICKY. doesn't matter

BIRD. course it matters – are you jealous?

NICKY. of what

BIRD. I had people waiting for me. Ready to whisk me away on a night out the minute they could.

NICKY. me too

BIRD. do they actually like you though. Like really

NICKY. yeah

BIRD. if you say so

NICKY. I do say so

BIRD. and what you say is the law, right?

NICKY. in here, yeah

,

BIRD. why are we here?

,

NICKY. four years after the state he was in

BIRD. ah I see

BIRD *downs his drink.*

Come on then. Get it over with

NICKY. four years after you'd finished with him

BIRD. who says we were finished with him

NICKY. doesn't really seem fair

BIRD. why do you care how long I got I didn't think fascists got involved in courts, thought you preferred extra-judicial means

NICKY. neither do you

BIRD. too bloody right

NICKY. but the police got to you first. They came and dragged you off the poor bastard

BIRD. 'poor bastard' oh fuck off with that

NICKY. I'm pretty sure they scooped up part of him and put it in a bin bag.

BIRD. that's not true

NICKY. they did they used a dustpan and brush to get part of him up

BIRD. no they didn't

NICKY. you weren't there for the mopping up.

BIRD. oh I'm sorry I know I should have thrown a benefit concert but it seemed like a good idea at the time you know

NICKY. I heard all about it

BIRD. I'm sure you did, it made the papers

NICKY. they told me all about it

BIRD. Did you read it in the papers? Can you even read?

NICKY. he was just walking down the street. On his way back from his shift. His poor girlfriend

BIRD. He was not just walking down the street.

NICKY. he was just walking down the street

BIRD. he was walking down the street with those tattoos on his skin. He was covered in them. With a shaved head. With red laces in his boots. That's not walking down the street it's just not

NICKY. he was harmless. He was a bin man

BIRD. with swastika tattoos. A bin man with swastika tattoos. If you have that uniform you can't complain when people react to it. Anything like that, if you make a spectacle of yourself you should expect a reaction

NICKY. you should expect to have the shit kicked out of you, you mean

BIRD. if you're a fascist then yes you should spend every second of your short lonely miserable life in total fucking terror.

NICKY. he lost an eye

BIRD. but he kept those tattoos didn't he.

,

I should have finished him off. He was still breathing. He shouldn't have been breathing when I was finished with him. It's the only way we win.

NICKY. have you lost then

BIRD. not yet

NICKY. I think you've lost

BIRD. we haven't lost

NICKY. even when it's right in front of you you've got no fucking clue

BIRD. what do you want. You could do anything you wanted to me. What are you waiting for – the British Movement's finest example of a clinical psychopath and yet

,

Oh. How long would you get if you did me in? Am I worth it? It'd be your what, third time?

NICKY. Fourth.

BIRD. what were the others it's hard for a girl to keep up

NICKY. there was a thing on a tube train. I got done for jumping up and down on someone's head. He stopped moving. He lived though. Maybe I'm not as good at this as you lot seem to think.

BIRD. someone said that thing at the cinema was yours

NICKY. it was but I didn't go down for that one

BIRD. what was the third?

NICKY. thing at a train station. Got me four years.

BIRD. anyone dead?

NICKY. two.

,

We didn't leave them breathing.

BIRD. clearly.

NICKY. they know what I can do

BIRD. yes

NICKY. that's why nobody asks questions. They don't need to. I don't need to prove anything.

BIRD. the fuck are you on about

NICKY. You've done your bit and still nobody cares about you. Or what you've done. You beat a man into the gutter till he went blind and nobody cares about you.

BIRD. I don't want fame

NICKY. fuck off

BIRD. I don't care

NICKY. everyone cares. Everyone wants to be watched.

BIRD. are you trying to shame me

NICKY. you think you're so much better than me

BIRD. I am

NICKY. where

BIRD. I saw a man turn into an animal once.

,

NICKY. did you really

BIRD. I did. His face got longer and his jaw came out here and his back curved over and his arms got longer and he got hair all over and his teeth grew out of his head and they got sharper. And then he took someone's face off with one bite.

NICKY. did he now

BIRD. you don't believe me

NICKY. I think it's a good story

BIRD. yeah I guess you would he didn't take your face off

NICKY. with one bite

BIRD. with one bite.

,

it's what they said about you

NICKY. what is

BIRD. 'worse than an animal'

NICKY. shut your fucking mouth I'm not an animal

BIRD. no, you're worse apparently

NICKY. Shut. Your fucking. Mouth

BIRD. I can still smell the blood on you.

,

I do what I do because beating you off the streets is the
only language your lot understand. The only thing that gets
through to you.

NICKY. I'm not actually thick

BIRD. funny way of showing it

NICKY. despite how everyone looks at me, all your lot, I'm not
actually thick

BIRD. All my lot?

NICKY. yeah like I haven't got a clue.

BIRD. then why do you do it

NICKY. It's my work

BIRD. work?

NICKY. exactly

BIRD. Not exactly the word I'd use. I'd call it mindless violence

NICKY. mindless?

BIRD. Senseless. Thoughtless.

NICKY. oh no. No I thought about it. I thought about it a lot.

BIRD. find that hard to believe

NICKY. You have to pick the right target.

BIRD. Family. The right family.

,

NICKY. yes sometimes that was the target

BIRD. With a child

NICKY. sometimes

BIRD. A nine-year-old

NICKY. sometimes that was the target

,

BIRD. it is Nicky, isn't it. That is your name.

NICKY. yeah

BIRD. are you proud of what you do, Nicky?

NICKY. course. It's important.

BIRD. Important?

NICKY. yeah

BIRD. you do important work with broken beer bottles thrust in the face of a kid

NICKY. black

,

BIRD. excuse me?

NICKY. I have to do it

BIRD. What for.

,

NICKY. this country. For British people.

BIRD. for white people.

NICKY. that's what I said

BIRD. by glassing everyone else off the streets

NICKY. it'll work

BIRD. do you think

NICKY. I know

BIRD. that's still not an answer, why did you do it

,

NICKY. For him. My God. My Führer.

,

BIRD. right

,

That's why we beat you off the streets. Because there's no way you can unlearn that. Maybe some people. But not you. Not after all those chances.

NICKY *laughs*.

NICKY. I'm special.

BIRD. Who was waiting for you when you got out? Anybody?

NICKY. have you seen yourself. Those jeans, Docs. Shame about the hair or you'd fit right in.

BIRD. what are you talking about

NICKY. even dressed like one of us

BIRD. don't flatter yourself sweetheart it's a cheap look.

NICKY. they still call you Bird?

BIRD. yeah

NICKY. fucking stupid

BIRD. we say it's short for Jailbird now

NICKY. what was it, your real name, Henry?

BIRD. and who cares what my name is I still got my hands dirty and I'd do it all again. See a Nazi, put a boot in his face.

,

Come on, big boy, what's your problem. You're normally chomping at the bit by now. Can't sustain a conversation for this long can you. Straight in with a glass to the face.

,

COME ON.

NICKY. who's with you

BIRD. who cares

NICKY. who knows?

BIRD. who knows what? That you're working security at a gay bar? Who cares?

NICKY. what have you seen

BIRD. I haven't seen anything I told you this is my first night out

NICKY. who have you seen me with

,

BIRD. oh you're fucking kidding me

NICKY. no –

BIRD. Not Nicky Crane a fucking poof

NICKY. nobody can know

BIRD. you work on the door so –

NICKY. I don't mean that do I

BIRD. no I'm sorry you cannot possibly be this stupid. No no no you really can't be this stupid it's not even funny it's not even interesting it's just quite... pathetic.

NICKY. watch it

BIRD. are you seriously a poof? This whole time?

NICKY. you need to be quiet

BIRD. oh you're terrified aren't you? They don't properly know do they? All your Nazi mates don't know

NICKY. they know I do security so it makes sense. Just a job

BIRD. fucking hell you're unbelievable

NICKY. it's a job

BIRD. so they don't know you really really like working here

NICKY. I do security.

BIRD. we all know what you are. We all know what you do

NICKY. I do / security

BIRD. I'm not talking about you being a fucking bouncer I'm talking about you being a fucking Nazi. And apparently a bender too.

,

Don't know why I'm surprised. Who was that bloke, one of yours, Colin Jordan. He was a bit fruity too, wasn't he?

NICKY. the fuck you mean fruity

BIRD. what was it he resigned over? Wasn't he shoplifting knickers. From a Tesco. In Coventry. It's you lot who are perverts.

NICKY. Nobody knows about me.

BIRD. do you get off with the clientele often?

,

NICKY. It's dark. Skins look like skins.

BIRD. Do you still go out queerbashing?

NICKY. no I don't

BIRD. what changed your mind

NICKY. no I never went queerbashing. Never let it happen in front of me either.

BIRD. how exceedingly generous of you.

,

They're gonna know. They probably already do. You know that.

NICKY. I fuck who I want and nobody tells me what to do. They know what I do when they try.

,

BIRD. which is what

NICKY. I hit them and I hit them and I hit them again

I hit them until it doesn't feel like hitting anything at all

I get blood spattered on me

It gets into my eyes and I try to rub the blood out of my eye but I end up rubbing the blood *into* my eye

I could do anything I wanted to you and nobody would notice would they I could do anything and it would be ages before your friends stop dancing to realise they haven't seen you in a while

BIRD. Course you could. I'm entirely at your mercy. So why are you still talking then. Because I could really do with another vodka soda.

NICKY. what do you think I'm gonna do

,

BIRD. I think you're going to let me go

NICKY. no

,

BIRD. This doesn't seem like your type, you seem like you'd prefer a Friday night crowd. They probably don't fight back.

NICKY. you don't know anything about

BIRD. are your ears burning, Nicky

NICKY. they don't gossip like you lot. They won't know.

BIRD. gossip gossip gossip. Everyone does it. Including your lot.

NICKY. They won't listen

BIRD. course they will

NICKY. they won't believe it

BIRD. Alright. But you've had me here for how long? I don't think you've got the stomach. I don't think you believe it. You can't put me down like an animal because you can't go back can you. You wouldn't cope.

,

let me go.

NICKY. I know what I am. And you're wrong.

BIRD. So let me go. Even now, you're just some poof trying to be a big boy. It doesn't work. Not with me. Not with so many other people. And I don't think you even notice. Listen to me. Fuck knows why I'm

,

There's a bar full of gays out there who just think you're a bit of rough. Really butch. They think being smacked around by you is a bit of fun. But far more importantly there's a load of fucking Nazis you think you're friends with. It won't protect you. Once they pay attention and realise what you are they'll hate you the same way they hate all the rest of us. The way they want us dead, they'll want you dead the same. And you've sided with them, and quite probably that'll kill us all.

,

If you were gonna have your way with me, you'd have done it by now. We both know that.

,

NICKY *unlocks the door. He holds it open for* BIRD.

NICKY. Have a nice night.

BIRD *laughs*.

BIRD. Thanks. Go fuck yourself sweetheart.

BIRD *leaves*.

NICKY *panics, he can't move*.

He retches, but there's nothing there.

FOUR

August 1990.

CHRISTOPHER *slides into the bathroom, clutching a
magazine. He slips into the cubicle, locks it behind him.*

,

NICKY *enters, knocks on the cubicle. He presses his ear to
the door –*

NICKY. what are you doing in there

Then he puts his shoulder to it – out comes CHRISTOPHER.

what are you doing you dirty bastard, that's a fucking bent
mag – didn't know you were a fucking queer

NICKY *pulls out a knife.* CHRISTOPHER *is on his knees.*

you're a fucking bastard I'm going to slit your fucking throat,
I fucking hate queers

NICKY *holds the knife to* CHRISTOPHER*'s throat.*

Lick my fucking boots.

CHRISTOPHER *starts licking* NICKY*'s boots.*

Yeah. You like that you dirty bent bastard?

CHRISTOPHER *moans in assent.*

While you've been wanking one out over your bent
magazines you wanna know what I've been doing?

NICKY *pulls out a (full) condom from his pocket.*

I've been fucking my girlfriend. I've been fucking my
girlfriend silly. You want some of this? You want this spunk
on your face?

NICKY *squeezes the contents of the condom over* CHRISTOPHER*'s face.*

Yeah you like that you bent bastard?

CHRIS. yeah, yeah, do you want to fuck me

NICKY. yeah I'll fuck you too as well you / bent bastard

CHRIS. Oh my god it's in my eye

NICKY. what

CHRIS. it's completely in my eye, no we have to stop we have to stop a second.

CHRISTOPHER *stands up, leaves.*

,

CHRISTOPHER *returns with a flannel, starts rubbing at his face.*

NICKY. you okay

CHRIS. No no I'm not do I look okay. How bad is my pinkeye going to be?

NICKY. what are you talking about

CHRIS. fucking stings.

NICKY. sorry

CHRIS. right, done. Have we got another condom?

NICKY *pulls out another (full) condom from his pocket.*

Oh good. Okay. So we'll go again, from the top I think. Oh, and when you do the bit with the knife, make sure, I mean the camera probably can't see so if you move to the side it's like a clearer view

NICKY. right

CHRIS. and then it's like knife, condom, neck, and it's all really clear for the camera

NICKY. okay

CHRIS. I know it's your first time and you're probably nervous or / whatever

NICKY. not nervous

CHRIS. oh please everyone gets stage fright sometimes I wouldn't worry, just be very aware of the fact that it's not really real. And that it's for the camera. Yeah?

,

NICKY. yeah

CHRIS. excellent, we're still rolling okay, après vous –

    CHRISTOPHER *ushers* NICKY *out of the bathroom.*

    And… go.

    CHRISTOPHER *slides into the bathroom, clutching a magazine. He slips into the cubicle, locks it behind him.*

    ,

    NICKY *enters, knocks on the cubicle. He presses his ear to the door –*

NICKY. what are you doing in there

    Then he puts his shoulder to it – out comes CHRISTOPHER.

    what are you doing you dirty bastard, that's a fucking bent mag – didn't know you were a fucking queer

    NICKY *pulls out a knife.* CHRISTOPHER *is on his knees.*

    you're a fucking bastard I'm going to slit your fucking throat, I fucking hate queers

    NICKY *holds the knife to* CHRISTOPHER*'s throat.*

    Lick my fucking boots.

    CHRISTOPHER *starts licking* NICKY*'s boots.*

    Yeah. You like that you dirty bent bastard?

    CHRISTOPHER *moans in assent.*

    While you've been wanking one out over your bent magazines you wanna know what I've been doing?

    NICKY *pulls out a (full) condom from his pocket.*

I've been fucking my girlfriend. I've been fucking my girlfriend silly. You want some of this? You want this spunk on your face?

NICKY *squeezes the contents of the condom over* CHRISTOPHER*'s face.*

Yeah you like that you bent bastard?

CHRIS. yeah, yeah, do you want to fuck me

NICKY. yeah I'll fuck you too as well you bent bastard

CHRIS. you can do anything you want to me, anything at all

NICKY. do you promise

CHRIS. anything you want I promise

NICKY. yeah you dirty bastard

CHRIS. (bent bastard)

NICKY. yeah you dirty bent bastard

CHRIS. are you gonna fuck me?

NICKY. yes I am

CHRIS. you're gonna fuck me!

NICKY. yes

CHRISTOPHER *grabs* NICKY*'s crotch.*

CHRIS. you're gonna fuck me?

NICKY. y- yes

CHRISTOPHER *feels around* NICKY*'s crotch for any sign of life.*

,

CHRIS. ah

NICKY. it's fine

,

CHRIS. have you tried thinking sexy thoughts

NICKY. I'll be fine just give me a sec

CHRIS. we can take a break if that's / helpful

NICKY. no no it's fine give me a minute

   ,

CHRIS. Nicky.

NICKY. sorry

CHRIS. no I don't think there's anything there is / there –

NICKY. sorry

   ,

   Think it was the stopping and starting again

CHRIS. yeah but there's lots of stopping and starting when you do this

NICKY. it was trying to remember the words I think I'm alright till I've got to do the words

CHRIS. right okay do you want to see if you can sort yourself out? I can give you a minute if that's helpful

NICKY. what do you mean

CHRIS. or maybe there's something else we can do in the meantime,

NICKY. like what

CHRIS. can you piss on cue?

NICKY. what

CHRIS. no that's an unfair ask off the cuff, you're probably not hydrated. Let me do some more boot stuff

   CHRISTOPHER *checks the camera is still going, then gets down on his knees and starts licking the boots again.*

   NICKY *looks faintly bored.*

   ,

   Anything?

NICKY. where'd you find this place?

CHRIS. just industrial wasteland isn't it

NICKY. right

   ,

CHRIS. Alright.

NICKY. sorry it's all

CHRIS. we'll just do some more filler.

NICKY. Filler?

CHRIS. yeah we'll get some shots of you looking all buff.

NICKY. what do I do

CHRIS. well I get out of the way and you just stand there.

NICKY. like this

CHRIS. shoulders back, chest out.

> NICKY *follows* CHRISTOPHER*'s instructions.*
> CHRISTOPHER *wipes his face again.*

Now to the side. Now your back.

> CHRISTOPHER *stifles a yawn.*

Other side. Okay face me again. Now try rubbing yourself or something.

> NICKY *does.*

> ,

This isn't going to happen, is it.

> ,

NICKY. Sorry / I

CHRIS. no it's just a waste of fucking time isn't it really

NICKY. I'm not normally like this

CHRIS. there's only so much rubbing you can do

> CHRISTOPHER *starts getting changed, pulling clothes out of a duffle bag.*

I do love my job, I really do, very lucky person, but I just wonder why I bother getting dressed up at all if there's no orgasm at the end of the day. Right, *shit*, I should have done this earlier, this is a waiver, basically just means that if we were to get raided that I'm not liable. And then I can use the boots stuff too.

CHRISTOPHER *gives* NICKY *a piece of paper.*

NICKY. raided

CHRIS. yes, raided

NICKY. right

CHRIS. Sign here.

CHRISTOPHER *points.* NICKY *signs.*

And cash –

He hands NICKY *a couple of notes.*

NICKY. thanks

CHRIS. it's fair for the work you've done

NICKY. okay yeah

,

do your mates know you do this

CHRIS. Yes they do. Half of them get off on it. Will you tell yours? I presume nobody knows you're here.

NICKY. no

CHRIS. they must know that you're into this though

NICKY. they don't

CHRIS. how do you get away with it?

NICKY. nobody asks me any questions

CHRIS. half of them probably do it themselves. Real market for this stuff.

NICKY. what do you mean

CHRIS. people love skinhead porn.

NICKY. oh right yeah

CHRIS. people must throw themselves at you. You're such a type. Skinhead, the Docs, it's a whole thing

NICKY. it's how I look

CHRIS. yeah course. But it's odd. No not odd, eccentric. One of those things that makes you proud to British.

NICKY. don't really think about it

CHRIS. It's probably good that you don't think about it. Some people take it so seriously though. Some people I work with take it really seriously.

NICKY. take what seriously

CHRIS. the look, and then the sex. They take the sex too seriously.

,

Oh you know

NICKY. no, I don't

,

CHRIS. They panic, 'it's not safe', they get all scared.

NICKY. why are they scared

CHRIS. Exactly! It should be fun. If you have to think about it too much it's gonna be... I don't know. Undercooked.

NICKY. what the fuck are you talking about

CHRIS. what the fuck are you smirking at?

NICKY. do you take it seriously

CHRIS. not really.

> NICKY *pulls on a T-shirt. It has a white nationalist slogan on it.*

right gorgeous, that was fun, we should do it again sometime. See if we can finish the job.

NICKY. what do you mean

CHRIS. we should do it again sometime. As long as you thought it was fun

NICKY. yeah I thought it was fun

CHRIS. was it convincing, do you think? Just a costume for me, isn't it. You, however. You're legitimate.

,

NICKY. Do you want to see me again?

CHRIS. yeah don't see why not

NICKY. so not like

,

So maybe if you wanted to go for a drink

,

CHRIS. what do you mean go for a drink. With you?

NICKY. just thought maybe you might want to go for a drink

CHRIS. um. No. No.

NICKY. no that's fine

CHRIS. it's just. It's not that I don't want to fuck you, I do that seems like it might be fun, but a fuck for the camera is not having a drink is it. How would that go, have you seen your tattoos?

NICKY. but you like my tattoos

CHRIS. for a porno, sure. The camera loves them. Not going to introduce you to my parents though am I

NICKY. you'll fuck me, but you won't go for a drink with me

CHRIS. I thought it was your everyday common or garden transgression. It's not like we'd even really bothered with names is it, I didn't know it wasn't just the look. And look I don't judge, I don't particularly care I'm friends with all sorts. But you forget I knew you were a queer long before I knew you were a fascist.

NICKY. I don't do it any more. Really, I don't do any of that stuff.

CHRIS. I'm not sure I trust you. I think you bleed through. I think this might not all be pretend for you. Your reputation precedes you.

NICKY. you don't know me

CHRIS. no but I know what you've done.

NICKY. and what's that

,

CHRIS. You're an actual fucking Nazi. And you're a proper poof. It seemed an interesting contradiction and then I realised it wasn't a contradiction to you at all. You fuck and get fucked by other men,

NICKY. and? And what? I fuck and get fucked by other men. So do you.

CHRIS. Don't get me wrong I'm not saying you've got to conform to some sissy stereotype. But this is something else entirely isn't it. I mean you just go to town on them don't you

NICKY. not queers. And I don't do it any more. I don't.

CHRIS. still don't know you're queer though do they

NICKY. I don't do any of that stuff, I believe in individualism

CHRIS. and the T-shirt, what's that. Real? Not real?

NICKY. the only clean one I had

CHRIS. Sure. Clean. Whatever. You might not do it anymore, but you wouldn't want anyone thinking you're a bent bastard now, would we?

NICKY *punches* CHRISTOPHER *square in the face.* CHRISTOPHER *goes down.* NICKY *kicks him once, twice, a third time.*

NICKY *rests his boot against the side of* CHRISTOPHER's *head.*

,

NICKY. I am not like you. I am not embarrassed. I fuck who I want and nobody tells me what to do because this is what I do when they try. Are you listening to this. I know what I am.

NICKY *releases* CHRISTOPHER.

CHRISTOPHER *drags himself to his feet. He stumbles to pick up his duffle bag, and then, slowly, leaves the bathroom.*

NICKY *watches him go.*

FIVE

November 1993.

A hospital bathroom. A curtain is drawn in front of a running shower.

CRAIG *cracks open the bathroom door.*

CRAIG. Nicky?

NICKY. Fuck off Craig.

CRAIG *closes the door behind him.*

CRAIG. oh so this is where you disappeared to is it, been looking all over for you

NICKY. don't let anyone in

CRAIG. I won't

NICKY. I mean it don't let anyone in

CRAIG. nobody's coming in.

CRAIG *looks, then goes behind the curtain.*

oh for *goodness* sake what are you playing at

NICKY. I'm on my moped what does it look like

CRAIG. you're ridiculous.

NICKY. I am busy

CRAIG. doing what?

CRAIG *turns the shower off.*

NICKY. I'm breaking them in

CRAIG. in the shower

NICKY. someone told me it helps

CRAIG *reappears, finds* NICKY*'s hospital gown and passes it through the curtain.*

CRAIG. make yourself decent

,

NICKY *draws the curtain. He's frail, and with his hospital gown he's wearing a pair of cherry-red Docs.*

Breaking them in?

NICKY. it helps.

CRAIG. we need to get you back to bed

NICKY. no

CRAIG. you need to rest you're exhausted

NICKY. I'm not going back there

CRAIG. You have to

NICKY. No I fucking don't have to go back there

CRAIG. it's the best place for you

NICKY. give me ten minutes. Ten minutes not on that fucking ward.

,

CRAIG. this is daft,

NICKY. Ten minutes.

CRAIG. Fine. Ten minutes.

,

NICKY. what are you just gonna stand there and watch me the whole time

CRAIG. I need to make sure that you're okay, you idiot

NICKY. I'm fine

CRAIG. yes you look it. Picture of health. You're panicking, just breathe

NICKY. why do you sound like my mum

CRAIG. calm down

NICKY. okay alright

They both take deep breaths. NICKY *feels a bit silly.*

CRAIG. feel better?

NICKY. fuck off

CRAIG. is that a yes?

NICKY. I'm fine. I mean like

CRAIG. I know what you mean by fine.

,

NICKY. can I tell you something

CRAIG. of course you can

NICKY. okay. I hate those fucking shorts.

CRAIG. oh right

NICKY. honestly I do I really hate them I'm sorry I hate those stupid fucking shorts

CRAIG. I'm only wearing them because I cycled here

NICKY. you look like a poof

CRAIG. thanks but I wore them as I walked into an AIDS ward and kissed one of the patients so I think something else might have given that away

NICKY. I could be an addict

CRAIG. I suppose so, are you an addict?

NICKY. no

CRAIG. then by a process of elimination you must be a haemophiliac

NICKY. oh fuck off

CRAIG. look like a poof she says yes but my arse does look *bona.*

,

And you look good too.

NICKY. Fuck off.

CRAIG. you do you look better

NICKY. you just went from saying I look good to 'better'?

CRAIG. oh come on

NICKY. better than what? What the fuck does better mean

CRAIG. You look older

NICKY. I don't want to look old

CRAIG. I didn't say you look old I said you look older, you're leaner it looks good on you

NICKY. but I look better right

CRAIG. you do

NICKY. mm. Fuck this.

CRAIG. we need to get you back to the ward

NICKY. not yet

CRAIG. Nicky come on don't be stupid

NICKY. I want my ten minutes

,

CRAIG. it's / just

NICKY. you're not winning this fucking argument I won't let you.

,

did I tell you about Martin

CRAIG. remind me which one's Martin

NICKY. the dancer

CRAIG. oh he's pretty

NICKY. yes fuck off

CRAIG. the pretty dancer sorry but that is easy to remember

NICKY. full body cast. Slipped into a coma

CRAIG. oh God what / happened

NICKY. he broke his back after nine months of vomiting. They don't think he's got very long left.

CRAIG. I'm sorry

NICKY. yeah well. It's

,

Craig I don't. I don't think I can walk. Back to the ward I don't

CRAIG. it's okay

NICKY. think I'm gonna be able to walk it

CRAIG. it's fine, it's fine

NICKY. it's not though it's really not

CRAIG. I can get the chair it'll / be fine

NICKY. no never mind I'll fucking walk

CRAIG. if you can't walk then you can't fucking walk

NICKY. I'm gonna stay here

CRAIG. you're what

NICKY. I'm gonna stay here.

,

CRAIG. and do what, lean?

NICKY. I'm gonna lean, yeah. I'm not getting in that chair again.

CRAIG. sorry would you rather we carried you

NICKY. honestly yes I would

CRAIG. fine I'll grab your legs. Someone else can get your arms. We'll swing you down the corridor.

NICKY. can I pick the other bloke

CRAIG. we're getting the chair

NICKY. we're fucking not

CRAIG. must you be so belligerent

NICKY. don't talk to me like I'm an idiot

> CRAIG *goes as if to get the chair.*

> I said I'm not doing the chair, didn't I

CRAIG. can you please just try not to argue with everything I say

NICKY. I know what I want

CRAIG. I'm not sure what you want is possible all of the time

NICKY. why's that

CRAIG. because sometimes it feels like you have no idea what's actually happening to you and other times it feels like you're aggressively pessimistic

NICKY. I know what's going on I know exactly what they're doing to me. You underestimate me everyone underestimates me

CRAIG. I don't underestimate you

NICKY. you do

CRAIG. no, no I don't

NICKY. yes you do.

,

I take two five-hundred milligrams of AZT twice a day. I have prescriptions for Rifater, Pyridoxine and Methenamine.

I spend a lot of time on a Folinic Acid drip. I take Triludan, Sulfadiazine and Carbamazepine. Do not act like I don't know what's happening to me

CRAIG. calm down

NICKY. I am fucking calm it's just fucking hot in here and I'm surrounded by what's going to happen to me in this place. Every day there's a brand-new way to find out how my body's going to screw me

CRAIG. you don't know that

NICKY. by this point yeah I think I do

CRAIG. you might be one of the lucky ones. All those drugs are new. You don't need to be like this it's not good for you to be thinking like this.

NICKY. yeah but it's everywhere, this is the only place that doesn't smell like death and that's because it smells like piss

CRAIG. it's not good for you

NICKY. I've thought about them all, all the ways my body could shut down on me

,

there's my eyes they're already going a bit funny so the blindness is going to happen

CRAIG. your eyes are doing what

NICKY. bit fuzzy

CRAIG. have you told the doctors

NICKY. basically it boils down to, I reckon I'll put up with the shits and the wasting and the blindness and the funny taste in my mouth but I'm not gonna do the dementia

CRAIG. stop it

NICKY. I mean it I just don't want the dementia. I don't want to go mad, smother me if I start going mad okay or find a cliff to push me off

CRAIG. Stop it.

NICKY. why still gonna die either way

CRAIG. I don't like this

NICKY. I'm not in the mood for a talk from you

CRAIG. it's not good for you

NICKY. it's really hot in here isn't it

CRAIG. I need you to be well I don't want you thinking / like this

NICKY. it is it's really hot

CRAIG. it's November

NICKY. don't you feel hot

> NICKY *rips off his hospital gown – there are KS lesions on his back.*

CRAIG. what are you doing

NICKY. I'm gonna melt

CRAIG. no you're not you'll freeze you're not well

> CRAIG *takes off his jacket and puts it around* NICKY.

> And we need to get you back to the ward

NICKY. no

> ,

> Do you really not feel hot?

CRAIG. No. No I don't.

> ,

NICKY. thank you for the jacket

CRAIG. you're welcome

> ,

NICKY. oh fuck

> *He crouches down to pick the gown up.*

CRAIG. you can't put it back on

NICKY. it'll be fine I'll just

CRAIG. You can't just put it back on, you muppet, it's been on the fucking floor

NICKY. it's punk right

CRAIG. Oh fuck off it's not punk it's bacteria it's probably riddled with whatever stuff lives on the floor of a hospital bathroom and you have no immune system so you can't afford to catch whatever it is that lives on the floor of a hospital bathroom

NICKY. you're a drama queen

CRAIG. You don't take it seriously

NICKY. it's already going to kill me why should I take it seriously

CRAIG *picks up the gown.*

CRAIG. I'll get you a new one.

,

NICKY. they say they'll let us wear our own clothes soon.

CRAIG. really?

NICKY. yeah someone on the ward said so

CRAIG. I still don't think they'll let you wear your boots in bed.

CRAIG *goes out.*

NICKY *is alone.*

He lowers the jacket and stares at himself in the mirror. Tries to reach around to touch the lesions on his back. Runs his hand over his stubbly scalp. He holds out his hand to see if it's shaking. It is.

CRAIG *comes back in with a clean gown.* NICKY *gently takes off the jacket.*

ready?

NICKY. yes

CRAIG. arms up

> NICKY *raises his arms.* CRAIG *slips the gown over his head.*

> NICKY *turns around so* CRAIG *can tie up the back.*

NICKY. Do people notice them, do you think

CRAIG. do people notice what

NICKY. the spots

> ,

CRAIG. Nicky you're covered in them

NICKY. yeah but do people notice them

> CRAIG *kisses the back of* NICKY *'s neck.*

CRAIG. yes I think they do

> ,

NICKY. sorry

CRAIG. Okay.

> ,

NICKY. not doing the chair

CRAIG. do you like being in pain

NICKY. no I really don't

CRAIG. sometimes it really does feel like you relish it

NICKY. well maybe it is what I deserve

CRAIG. this isn't a punishment

NICKY. it feels like a punishment

CRAIG. no I'm not doing this again, it is not a punishment for what you've done and those tattoos it's not a punishment for your sins or your crimes, it's not sent down from God it's not a biological trait or inherited it's not your past coming home to roost it's a virus. It's a virus that you've got and that has opened the door to illness and cancers and fungus and everything else and yes it's fucking awful but it is not a punishment. It is not something you deserve. Or can be sentenced to. What, we find the defendant guilty and we sentence him to AIDS.

NICKY. you don't know what they're like don't give them ideas

CRAIG. it's not a punishment Nicky

NICKY. You don't know what it is nobody does. But it's real

CRAIG. yes

NICKY. and I can't, like, I can't get away from it

,

CRAIG. if someone wanted you punished there are other ways

NICKY. that are worse than this?

CRAIG. it's not a punishment. it's just not

,

NICKY. you look exhausted

CRAIG. and I thought everyone looked good in bathroom lighting. I haven't been sleeping well

NICKY. Do you wanna swap? Try the ward for a change?

CRAIG. I'll pass

NICKY. The sheets come in two options, scratch or scratchier. I swear they're taking the skin off my arse

CRAIG. I didn't know they did exfoliation on the NHS

NICKY. they did what

CRAIG. nothing

NICKY. Why haven't you been sleeping well? You'd always be out like a light

CRAIG. Worry. And

,

NICKY. And what

CRAIG. Just not feeling that great

NICKY. What do you mean not feeling great

CRAIG. Night sweats

,

NICKY. What like bad night sweats

CRAIG. I've been waking up with them

NICKY. You should see a doctor, I've got plenty of them I can lend you one

CRAIG. No

NICKY. You need to see a doctor

CRAIG. Nicky I don't need to see a doctor we both know what the doctor would say

,

NICKY. but if it's early then

CRAIG. doesn't matter does it it doesn't matter

NICKY. maybe there's things that they can do

CRAIG. babe stop it

NICKY. did I do this

CRAIG. who cares

NICKY. I care.

CRAIG. This is why I wasn't. It wouldn't make a difference. And it doesn't belong to you. You can't give it to me. It's not yours.

,

NICKY. I didn't know that it / would

CRAIG. No. You didn't. Neither did I. And I can't have you worrying about me. I need you better.

,

NICKY. better

CRAIG. yes

,

NICKY. Okay

CRAIG. Come on, we need to get you back

There's a knock on the door.

NICKY. you said nobody / would

CRAIG. it's fine it's fine –

CRAIG *opens the door to a* NURSE *with a wheelchair.*

NICKY. oh absolutely fucking not

NURSE. right come on Nicky let's get you back to bed

NICKY. are you all fucking deaf or something? you can't make me I'm not finished

NURSE. nobody's trying to rush you, we're trying to help

NICKY. did you get him in here?

CRAIG. I said you might, we might need some help

NICKY. what 'Nicky can't use his legs any more'

NURSE. nobody's saying that but there's help here and you should take it

NICKY. I don't want your fucking help

CRAIG. Nicky please

NICKY. I don't fucking want this

NURSE. You're going to make yourself sick getting worked up like this

NICKY. I'm going to? *Going to?* He can fuck off, fuck right off, you hate me you all fucking hate me

NURSE. Nicky I don't have time to hate you, I'm too busy wiping your arse.

NICKY. I have told you I have told you so many fucking times what I want and you ignore me you just fucking ignore me

CRAIG *turns to the* NURSE –

CRAIG. would you just, give us a sec

,

Nicky –

NICKY. No.

CRAIG. That's your ten minutes.

NICKY. / Craig –

CRAIG. If you get in the chair now and you let him push you then you can get out of it just before we get to the ward and I'll help you the rest of the way. Let me look after you.

,

NICKY. fine

NICKY *lowers himself into the chair, holding on to* CRAIG *for support. The* NURSE *gives* CRAIG *a look unseen by* NICKY.

,

what

CRAIG. Boots.

NICKY. please don't make me

CRAIG. come on.

,

NICKY *unlaces his boots, pulls them off his feet, batting away* CRAIG*'s offer of help. He clutches them to his chest.*

NICKY. Happy?

CRAIG. Are you ready?

,

NICKY. I'm

,

yes

,

NURSE. Okay. Off we go.

The NURSE *pushes the chair out of the bathroom.* CRAIG *follows.*

,

The bathroom, at last, stands empty.

End.

Acknowledgments

My deepest thanks to the friends and collaborators who read, listened to me endlessly talk about, or otherwise helped get this play to the stage: Matthew Baldwin, Florence Bell, Jess Tucker Boyd, Jonathan Chan, Amy Crighton, Carrie Croft, Conor Dye, Deborah Halsey, Maddie Hindes, Tomas Howells, Benjamin Isaac, Keanu Adolphus Johnson, Tania Khan, Neil McPherson, Corey Montague-Sholay, David Segun Olowu, Nitin Parmar, Jake Richards, William Robinson, Akshay Sharan, Sophie Swithinbank, Pam Tait, Neal Tank, Charlotte Vickers, Kishore Walker, Joseph Winer.

And Matthew Iliffe, most of all.

H.M.
March 2024

A Nick Hern Book

Foam first published in Great Britain as a paperback original in 2024 by Nick Hern Books Limited, The Glasshouse, 49a Goldhawk Road, London W12 8QP, in association with Finborough Theatre and Croft & Dye Productions

Foam copyright © 2024 Harry McDonald

Cover photography by Ali Wright, designed by Matthew Iliffe

Designed and typeset by Nick Hern Books, London
Printed in Great Britain by Mimeo Ltd, Huntingdon, Cambridgeshire PE29 6XX

A CIP catalogue record for this book is available from the British Library

ISBN 978 1 83904 332 1